How to Manipulate People to Do Anything You Want

By

Perez Dalton

Table of Contents

Introduction 6

The Manipulation Practices 8

Improve Your Charm 14

Master The Emotions 16

Logic vs. Emotions 18

Use Physical Appearance 21

Play The Victim Card 23

Read Body Language 26

Fear and Relief 28

Other books by the Same Author 31

Disclaimer: Although manipulation is not necessarily a bad thing, the purpose of this book is not just to teach you how to manipulate people but to make you understand the ways of the manipulators clearly. It is very important to know whether you are being manipulated by someone, because some of the manipulation techniques are subtle and could be used on you for many years without you even noticing. Financial and emotional benefits of having he knowledge of these manipulation techniques are priceless. Your interaction will be modified and you will improve the quality of people you keep around. You will easily spot the fake ones, and create a space for the good ones to stay around you.

Other books by the same author:

Below are other books I also believe will help you in developing yourself physically and emotionally. There are powerful messages and principles to live by. Add these books to your library:

1. How to Be a Badass and Stop Doubting Yourself: The Ultimate Guide to Greatness, Power and Awesome Life (Self Improvement Plan)

2. How to Be Good At Everything: Develop a Good Memory, Succeed Where Others Fail, And Maximize Your Happiness. Create an Aura of Confidence!

3. How to Start Overcoming Fear, Right Now: 44 Powerful Ways of Gaining New Confidence, Developing a Positive Mindset and Reaching Your Dreams

4. How to Transform Your Life in 30 Days: Start Living Differently, Gain Emotional Freedom, and Attract Positive Relationships

5. How to Overcome Fear of Public Speaking (Glassophobia): Powerful Techniques for Creating Strong Social Presence, Staying Above Social Anxiety and Building Confidence

6. The 48 Laws of Leadership: Uncovered Strategies Used by Great Leaders to Achieve Success and Long-Term Dominance

7. How to Overcome Procrastination and Get Stuff Done: Stop Laziness and Perfectionism with These Powerful Life Strategies (Become Proactive)

8. How to Deal with Angry People Without Strangling Them to Death

9. 45 Killer Actions to Boost Your Self-Confidence: Ultimate Secrets for Building Self-Esteem and Thriving Socially

10. How to Overcome Worry & Start Living: Smart Ways to Deal with Negative Persistent Thoughts, Relieve Anxiety, Gain Confidence, & Live Stress-Free Life

Introduction

You don't need to settle for disappointment every time people say "no" to the things you really WANT. Apparently there are hundreds of ways to make people do stuff for you without having to beg or pay for their actions. Good manipulators are great leaders who are able to achieve their interests despite strong oppositions coming from different directions of life.

They don't accept 'no' for an answer and even when they seem to accept it, they create another path to make people do stuff. This book has brought to light the essence of manipulation and how to use it to get what you want. Starting from cultivating a better relationship to elevating yourself, business or career-wise, the techniques provided in this book are well-tested and work effectively in specific circumstances.

You will have the leverage to make even the people above you do what you want, pushing yourself toward victory in every endeavor. You will achieve your heart desire and every step you take will become significant to yourself and the people around you.

The Manipulation Practices

Conceal Evil in Altruism

Evil has to be concealed by good initial actions. If you are planning the offensive against a party, do not act negatively or even criticize in order to avoid raising a red flag. Do not pick a fight or blame them for the things they have done wrong. If possible, practically praise them and show them how much you love and care about their interests. With this they won't hate you and they will come closer, but only closer to the danger of your plan.

You need to make them feel like you are helping them. Even when they see the negativity in your actions. Paint your harsh actions with the illusion of tough love, by which they should continue to submit to your suggestions regardless how unpleasant. Apology can bring down their flag of rebellion, even as you continue to find ways to manipulate their interests.

The aim is to make them act and towards a direction you so desire. Let them feel cared for and that you love them too much, hence the negative actions. In the mean time you can always ask them about what you can do to help them. With this, you will get them by your side and you can easily influence them to run towards your interests. You will also maintain power and control over them, making sure that they become emotional about their commitment to your interest.

Overcome Doubt and Heal Trust Issues

At some point people may begin to doubt your intentions or motivation. It is your job to regain trust ad make sure that they are clear about the things you want, even when they have to believe the wrong thing. A lot of people have passed through manipulations especially in relationships, and as a result they tend to be sensitive to red flags.

Even when you are totally honest, some will doubt you; what more if you are not really honest with your intentions? You have to scratch really hard and be conscious of the things you display in the physical that will affect your output. One of the best ways people create trust amidst audience that have trust issues is to share some personal experiences that everyone can relate.

People tend to trust other people that have passed through the same experiences in some way. Humans are easily influenced by commonality. They want to feel the connection before they can trust you. Work hard in creating that connection and revamp it from time to time in order to keep winning.

Another way to build trust is to ask them for help about something personal, maybe a problem to solve. Make them feel like you are sharing your weak side, that you trust them. Automatically you will turn the table and they will begin to trust you in return.

You have to be a great actor if you want people to trust you, even when your truth is not a total truth. Instead of feeling the doubt within yourself, make sure you turn the table by making them uncomfortable in such a way they will begin to question their doubts toward you.

It is also important to learn about the things they lack and the things they desire the most. Be the ultimate source of their desire and make sure you can provide their needs in one way or the other. Be the source of motivation progress in their lives. Bring about the idea that saves the day, assume authority in a certain niche and make them depend on you even as you become reliable to a certain level.

Manipulation is not about negativity. In fact, the greatest manipulators use positivity to get people on the hook, and preserve the negativity until when they are in control of everything. To maintain your effectiveness, you have to create a balance between negativity and positivity, where positivity will always outweigh the other.

Improve Your Charm

Flirt and Flirt

Charming is synonymous to 'irresistible.' You cannot become charming if you are not attractive. Your personality and attitude has to be attractive before you can get the attention of people to discover that you are also charming. One of the ways to maintain charm and to keep people on their toes is by consistent flirting.

When you are recognized as the charming individual you will be treated with grace and your emotions will be well-taken care of. But part of being charming is being able to control your emotions and only channel them effectively. You don't have to react to everything, and when other people tend to fret over new situations, you have to remain calm even when deep within you are also scared.

Work as hard as possible to make them like you, by making them feel some emotional connection to you even when you are meeting for the first time. Flirt as much as possible and make sure that they respond positively. Flirting also suggest that you like the person. If you are charming and a flirt, they will be glad and would like to respond positively so they don't disappoint you.

Master The Emotions

We all understand that people everyday show lesser control over emotions. More people are poor when it comes to channeling the common emotions into something greater. If you want to truly manipulate people, go through their emotions. But the most important thing is to be able to master your own emotions. You have to know when outburst is effective and when being silent is even better.

There are different ways you can channel anger or at least pretend you are angry, disappointed, depressed, or happy just to manipulate how people feel about you. Sympathy, respect, fear, empathy, can be incited using different kinds of expressions of the emotions. But you have to be careful not to do the emotional acting excessively so people will not start doubting you.

Once you build trust, do not take the risk of shattering it because it will be hard to build it back especially when the people in question figured out that you've been manipulating them several times. So, work every day in mastering your own emotions using different situations as reference. It may take time for this to happen but once achieved, most of the manipulations will turn out to be easier.

Logic vs. Emotions

Be fast in making people do stuff. Do not allow them to think too much. Stimulate their emotion then strike hard in turning their directions or actions. Logical choices demand seconds of thoughts and you might miss the goal. If you want people to act in a certain fashion that will prove beneficial to you, you have lodge a subtle attack over their emotions.

You will get them to do stuff faster and they won't ask too many questions. Things get easy when emotions are involved. With this you create a better insight, which would allow you to use empathy as a way of manipulating people to stay on your side all the time.

Bribery

Bribe someone materially or emotionally to make them feel the need to return the favor. You don't need to demand for a favor immediately, but making them feel like you are doing them a favor will make them your subjects and you will get them on your side every time—to be around when you need their inputs. Also, do not bribe them completely, make sure you show them that they could get a lot more inasmuch as they are willing to prove their loyalty to you.

The bribery doesn't have to cost you much. In fact, emotional bribery is the best, which comes free. It doesn't have to be a direct gift for nothingness. You can reward them for doing something great in order to encourage them to do something within your interests next time.

How do you bribe them?

Firstly, you have to figure out what the target really wants. Secondly, find a way to give them what they really want. Thirdly, give them the impression that they would have to give you something in return, even if not immediately. Let them know that you are not blackmailing them, that you are just doing your best to impress them, with the aim and need to get impressed in return.

Use Physical Appearance

Physical appearance is very important when it comes to assessment in the workplace and within the dating circle. Regardless of the brain behind the looks, good looks take away 60 percent of our attention most of the time. You don't need to be the opposite gender to manipulate the other. All you have to do is to look good, and everyone will have better respect for you.

Automatically the human brain thinks that better looking people are more intelligent. So they would expect smart decisions from you, and better ideas. If you are good looking, you have to learn better ways to put yourself out there and make your looks work for you even as you improve personally and professionally.

Even with the looks you have to be highly positive. You have to look welcoming before people will actually approach you. In order to keep people, you have to be cheering and motivating. You have to be the one that talks about hope amidst a group of hopeless individuals. This way you will make people feel good about themselves, even as you grow your self-confidence to the highest possible peak. No, you don't have to be perfect. Show your vulnerable side as well, but only as an attempt to make people feel better, that they can be useful to you as well.

Play The Victim Card

Playing the victim card will get you the attention you want, the sympathy and everything that comes after that. But you have to be careful not to do it excessively because you can easily get caught. Many people have used this technique that it has become the most common trick for manipulation, but it is still effective once done smartly and subtly.

Make Them Feel Guilty

Wait for a chance for someone to make a mistake, then make them feel guilty about everything. Once a person feels guilty he will try as much as possible to do the right thing next time. They will make an effort to create work where there is none just to make things right. This is where you will use the opportunity to suggest what they could do to make things right.

You can tell them exactly what you want them to do, and they will do it just to feel good again. In this case you don't need to tell them directly the things you need. Just go subtly even as you go in circles about the things you want. Subconsciously they will go with the flow, and that is when you will intensify your demand. Some people feel guilty immediately things go wrong around them, some don't take blame easily.

So the success of this technique will ultimately depends on the kind of person on target. Also, your experiences in subtle suggestions will also play a vital role on the amount of action that will be taken towards fulfilling your heart desire. This trick has been best used on relatives and friends who have once let you down; now they feel guilty and have to you remind them of the incident.

Read Body Language

Every good manipulator has to learn how to read body language and its social effect. Put focus on how people act when a word is being said or when they want to say something. Understand when their words are betraying their confidence. Even though the knowledge of the victim's emotional and psychological makeup would be important, being really observant will be helpful in figuring out people effectively.

One way to prove perfection is by relating on several occasions how the arms, the shoulders or the eyes rare being used. Thus you will actualize the feelings of such individual without them uttering a word. Also, emotional response can be recognized easily if you can read body language. This will demand more carefulness when it comes to observation and conclusion on the type of emotion being observed. You can bring in emotional manipulation in this case, leveraging your ability to read body language.

Fear and Relief

This is a popular technique for manipulation which has been used effectively by some of the best manipulators in history. Emotions are being put into test and as a result anxiety and stress are being inflicted on the victim. This is about making sure that the person has reached "over the edge" and about to fall off, then you can bring them down, and make sure they cool off.

Artificially inflicted mood swings can make people decide fast on things they don't really want. Instead of using their logics to make decisions or take actions, they impulsively go in the direction of their feelings and emotions, just to make the overwhelming feeling go away. In this case their emotion is at your mercy, and only you will know the extent of manipulation you could achieve.

For example, if a partner did some wrong, the manipulative partner may decide not listen to the reasons or apologies offered to them. Instead he pushes the victim to the wall by making them feel even worse about the bad feeling to the point of close breakage, then he tells them to calm down and that they are forgiven. In that case the victim may be willing to do anything just to fill up the space and make the bad experience go away.

So the technique is all about making people feel bad about what they did in an attempt to use their wrongs against them. If they don't feel bad enough, they will surely not take a step towards apologetic errands to satisfy the manipulator.

Other books by the Same Author

1. How to Be a Badass and Stop Doubting Yourself: The Ultimate Guide to Greatness, Power and Awesome Life (Self Improvement Plan)

2. How to Be Good At Everything: Develop a Good Memory, Succeed Where Others Fail, And Maximize Your Happiness. Create an Aura of Confidence!

3. How to Start Overcoming Fear, Right Now: 44 Powerful Ways of Gaining New Confidence, Developing a Positive Mindset and Reaching Your Dreams

4. How to Transform Your Life in 30 Days: Start Living Differently, Gain Emotional Freedom, and Attract Positive Relationships

5. How to Overcome Fear of Public Speaking (Glassophobia): Powerful Techniques for Creating Strong Social Presence, Staying Above Social Anxiety and Building Confidence

6. The 48 Laws of Leadership: Uncovered Strategies Used by Great Leaders to Achieve Success and Long-Term Dominance

7. How to Overcome Procrastination and Get Stuff Done: Stop Laziness and Perfectionism with These Powerful Life Strategies (Become Proactive)

8. How to Deal with Angry People Without Strangling Them to Death

9. 45 Killer Actions to Boost Your Self-Confidence: Ultimate Secrets for Building Self-Esteem and Thriving Socially

10. How to Overcome Worry & Start Living: Smart Ways to Deal with Negative Persistent Thoughts, Relieve Anxiety, Gain Confidence, & Live Stress-Free Life

www.ingramcontent.com/pod-product-compliance
Lightning Source LLC
Chambersburg PA
CBHW031517210526
45464CB00007B/2946